ORDINARY GRATITUDE

*CYCLE C SERMONS FOR
PENTECOST 23 THROUGH
CHRIST THE KING
BASED ON THE GOSPEL TEXTS*

MOLLY F. JAMES

CSS PUBLISHING COMPANY, INC.
LIMA, OHIO

ORDINARY GRATITUDE

FIRST EDITION
Copyright © 2015
by CSS Publishing Co., Inc.

Published by CSS Publishing Company, Inc., Lima, Ohio 45807. All rights reserved. No part of this publication may be reproduced in any manner whatsoever without the prior permission of the publisher, except in the case of brief quotations embodied in critical articles and reviews. Inquiries should be addressed to: CSS Publishing Company, Inc., Permissions Department, 5450 N. Dixie Highway, Lima, Ohio 45807.

Scripture quotations are from the New Revised Standard Version of the Bible. Copyright 1989 by the Division of Christian Education of the National Council of the Churches of Christ in the USA, Nashville, Thomas Nelson Publishers © 1989. Used by permission. All rights reserved.

Library of Congress Cataloging-in-Publication Data

James, Molly (Molly F.)
   Ordinary gratitude : Cycle C sermons for Pentecost 23 through Christ the King based on the gospel texts / Molly James. -- FIRST EDITION.
      pages cm
   ISBN 0-7880-2817-0 (alk. paper)
   1. Bible. Gospels--Sermons. 2. Sermons, American--21st century. 3. Pentecost season--Sermons. 4. Church year sermons. 5. Common lectionary (1992). Year C. I. Title.

BS2555.54.J355 2014
252'.64--dc23

2014037539

For more information about CSS Publishing Company resources, visit our website at www.csspub.com, email us at csr@csspub.com, or call (800) 241-4056.

e-book
ISBN-13: 978-0-7880-2818-2
ISBN-10: 0-7880-2818-9

ISBN-13: 978-0-7880-2817-5
ISBN-10: 0-7880-2817-0   PRINTED IN USA

*To my children, Katherine and Halsted,
who teach and inspire me to be more faithful.*

This is the first title written by Molly James for CSS Publishing Company, Inc.

Other titles for Cycle C available through CSS are:

God With Skin On
Advent/Christmas/Epiphany
Cycle C Gospel Texts
by Susan R. Andrews

Can I Get Some Help Over Here?
Lent/Easter
Cycle C Gospel Texts
by R. Robert Cueni

Spirit Works
Pentecost Day through Proper 12
Cycle C Gospel Texts
by Robert C. Cochran

Counting the Cost
Proper 13 through Proper 22
Cycle C Gospel Texts
by George Reed, O.S.L.

Ordinary Gratitude
Proper 23 through Christ the King Sunday
Cycle C Gospel Texts
by Molly F. James

Table of Contents

Proper 23 / Pentecost 21 / Ordinary Time 28   7
   Healing
   Luke 17:11-19; 2 Timothy 2:8-15

Proper 24 / Pentecost 22 / Ordinary Time 29   13
   Keeping the Faith
   Luke 18:1-8; 2 Timothy 3:14—4:5

Proper 25 / Pentecost 23 / Ordinary Time 30   19
   Reflecting God's Abundant Love
   Luke 18:9-14; 2 Timothy 4:6-8, 16-18

Proper 26 / Pentecost 24 / Ordinary Time 31   27
   Making a Difference
   Luke 19:1-10; 2 Thessalonians 1:1-4, 11-12

Proper 27 / Pentecost 25 / Ordinary Time 32   33
   Thy Will Be Done
   Luke 20:27-38; 2 Thessalonians 2:1-5, 13-17

Proper 28 / Pentecost 26 / Ordinary Time 33   39
   The Time Is Near
   Luke 21:5-19; 2 Thessalonians 3:6-13

Christ the King Sunday   45
Proper 29 / Pentecost 27 / Ordinary Time 34
   Christ's Monarchy
   Luke 23:33-43; Colossians 1:11-20

Reformation Day   51
   The Definition of Church
   John 8:31-36; Romans 3:19-28

All Saints Day 57
    Bless the World
  Luke 6:20-31; Ephesians 1:11-23

Thanksgiving Day 65
    An Attitude of Gratitude
  John 6:25-35; Philippians 4:4-9

Proper 23 / Pentecost 21 / Ordinary Time 28
Luke 17:11-19

On the way to Jerusalem Jesus was going through the region between Samaria and Galilee. As he entered a village, ten lepers approached him. Keeping their distance, they called out, saying, "Jesus, Master, have mercy on us!" When he saw them, he said to them, "Go and show yourselves to the priests." And as they went, they were made clean. Then one of them, when he saw that he was healed, turned back, praising God with a loud voice. He prostrated himself at Jesus' feet and thanked him. And he was a Samaritan. Then Jesus asked, "Were not ten made clean? But the other nine, where are they? Was none of them found to return and give praise to God except this foreigner?" Then he said to him, "Get up and go on your way; your faith has made you well."

* * *

2 Timothy 2:8-15

Remember Jesus Christ, raised from the dead, a descendant of David — that is my gospel, for which I suffer hardship, even to the point of being chained like a criminal. But the word of God is not chained. Therefore I endure everything for the sake of the elect, so that they may also obtain the salvation that is in Christ Jesus, with eternal glory. The saying is sure: If we have died with him, we will also live with him; if we endure, we will also reign with him; if we deny him, he will also deny us; if we are faithless, he remains faithful — for he cannot deny himself. Remind them of this, and warn them before God that they are to avoid wrangling over words, which does no good but only ruins those who are listening. Do your best to present yourself to God as one approved by him, a worker who has no need to be ashamed, rightly explaining the word of truth.

Proper 23 / Pentecost 21 / Ordinary Time 28
Luke 17:11-19
2 Kings 5:1-3, 7-15c; Psalm 111; 2 Timothy 2:8-15

Healing

When I was in fourth or fifth grade, I was helping my dad in the kitchen. I had been taught how to use a knife properly, but I wasn't always perfect at it. I slipped and nicked my finger. It was just a small cut but it was on the knuckle, so if the cut was going to heal, we had to find a way to splint my finger. I remember being very proud that my dad simply took a piece of kindling, cut off two small pieces, bandaged my finger, and taped it with adhesive tape. *Voila!* Within a matter of minutes I was on the road to healing. My finger healed quickly and you can't even see a scar. It is as if it never happened.

I think we often wish more of life were like that. When we are sick or injured, we hope and pray for healing. We want a transformation. We want our health completely restored. We want it to be as though we were never sick or hurt in the first place. We want transformation as we see in our scriptures today.

In 2 Kings we hear the story of Naaman, the army commander, who was healed from leprosy when he finally followed the instructions of the prophet Elisha and went to bathe in the River Jordan seven times. Amusingly, Naaman was initially resistant to this source of healing as he expected a great fanfare or an endurance trial or challenge in order to be healed rather than merely bathing in the Jordan. Yet that was not what was required of him. When he finally followed

Elisha's instructions, at the urging of the servants, Naaman was made clean. And this was some cleansing. It was not just that Naaman was healed of his leprosy, his flesh was completely restored to what it was before. He had the skin of a young boy after he bathed. Naaman got exactly what we wish for — complete healing and transformation.

Then in Luke's gospel we get another story of a miraculous healing of lepers. The ten lepers asked Jesus to have mercy on them. Jesus told them to go show themselves to the priests, and Jesus granted their wish, and "poof," just like that, they were healed. The leprosy was gone. Again, just what we wish for when we are the ones who are afflicted.

I have to admit, I actually have a hard time with these miraculous healing stories in the Bible. I find them rather frustrating. Because while the small cuts and bruises of life do heal over, the major experiences of pain and suffering in our lives do not disappear in an instant. Even when we are healed, the scars, the aftereffects of our treatments, the memories of our traumas remain. For most of us, healing, when it does happen, doesn't look anything like the stories we have in our scriptures this morning. And, of course, we can also think of those times when the healing doesn't happen — or at least not the way we think it should. Those times when we fervently prayed for a very different outcome than the one we got.

Those are the moments when we want to question God and perhaps even yell at God. We want to say "God, why do you give us these stories of perfect miraculous healing in our scriptures, but then you don't heal my brother, my mother, my child?" When we feel that way, we want to rail at and curse God. And well we should. Life feels completely unfair. And we are in good company being angry at God. The psalmist was frequently angry at God. Moses got angry at God. The Israelites were angry at God. One of my favorite Anglican thinkers, C.S. Lewis, got very angry at God when his wife died. It is okay to *be* angry at God — especially when we have experienced an outcome far different than what we were hoping for. What is not helpful, though, is to *stay* angry at God. Because staying angry at God only serves to deepen our own suffering, and it is a sign that we are too narrow in our focus.

Yes, there are stories like today's scriptures of miraculous healing that are rarely realized in our own lives. But note I said rarely and *not* never. Miraculous healings do happen. If we are paying attention, we will see them. I can personally attest. I was born twelve weeks prematurely with a 50% chance of survival. And here I am today. When I was thirteen, I was diagnosed with bone cancer and given a 70% chance of survival. And here I am today. And I am sure you can attest to miracles that have happened in your lives. Miracles do happen. Just not always how or when we want.

Most importantly, we must remember that not all stories of healing and transformation in the scriptures happen as they did for Naaman in 2 Kings or the lepers in Luke's gospel. Jacob was injured when he wrestled with the angel and he walked with a limp. The resurrected Jesus still has his wounds. Transformation and healing can happen even when things don't go perfectly, even when things are not brought back to the way they were before.

In fact, it is a central — if not *the* — central tenet of our Christian faith that God brings *new* life out of brokenness. That is exactly what Holy Week and Easter are all about. The harsh realities of Good Friday are about as broken and painful as one can get. But then comes Easter. Then comes God's affirmation to us that death, pain, and suffering do not have the last word. Love does. New life can come out of the most broken and painful moments in our lives.

We Christians are invited to always be on the lookout for how the brokenness of our lives can be transformational. I invite you, particularly if you are struggling or have struggled with challenges in your life — if there is brokenness or pain, illness, or injury — to take on a commitment to engage with that brokenness and seek after new ways of understanding it. In seeing our brokenness as a source of transformation, as a place out of which to share God's healing love with the world, we can live lives that affirm the beautiful truth that is at the heart of our faith: the conviction that the love of God is stronger than anything and everything in our world — even brokenness and death.

Come, let us journey together and build up hope. Amen.

Proper 24 / Pentecost 22 / Ordinary Time 29
Luke 18:1-8

Then Jesus told them a parable about their need to pray always and not to lose heart. He said, "In a certain city there was a judge who neither feared God nor had respect for people. In that city there was a widow who kept coming to him and saying, 'Grant me justice against my opponent.' For a while he refused; but later he said to himself, 'Though I have no fear of God and no respect for anyone, yet because this widow keeps bothering me, I will grant her justice, so that she may not wear me out by continually coming.' " And the Lord said, "Listen to what the unjust judge says. And will not God grant justice to his chosen ones who cry to him day and night? Will he delay long in helping them? I tell you, he will quickly grant justice to them. And yet, when the Son of Man comes, will he find faith on earth?"

* * *

2 Timothy 3:14—4:5

But as for you, continue in what you have learned and firmly believed, knowing from whom you learned it, and how from childhood you have known the sacred writings that are able to instruct you for salvation through faith in Christ Jesus. All scripture is inspired by God and is useful for teaching, for reproof, for correction, and for training in righteousness, so that everyone who belongs to God may be proficient, equipped for every good work.... In the presence of God and of Christ Jesus, who is to judge the living and the dead, and in view of his appearing and his kingdom, I solemnly urge you: proclaim the message; be persistent whether the time is favorable or unfavorable; convince, rebuke, and encourage, with the utmost patience in teaching. For the time is coming when people will not put up with sound doctrine, but having itching ears, they will accumulate for themselves teachers to suit their own desires, and will turn away from listening to the truth and wander away to myths. As for you, always be sober, endure suffering, do the work of an evangelist, carry out your ministry fully.

Proper 24 / Pentecost 22 / Ordinary Time 29
Luke 18:1-8
Genesis 32:22-31; Psalm 121; 2 Timothy 3:14-4:5

Keeping the Faith

Our Collect, our lessons — particularly the gospel and the epistle — are about being faithful, about being steadfast in our faith. In the gospel, "Jesus told his disciples a parable about their need to pray always and to not lose heart." Jesus went on to tell the parable of the unjust judge and the widow who was faithful and persistent, who did not give up in seeking justice, and finally her faith was rewarded. The letter to Timothy also tells us to be persistent and to keep the faith, to hold fast to its truths through thick and thin.

"Keep the faith." It is a great saying. It looks good on T-shirts and bumper stickers. It is easy to say to ourselves and others: "Just keep the faith." But it is much harder to do. I will confess that I find it very hard to do. You're probably thinking, well that is not very helpful. If the minister, the person who is meant to exemplify faith, who is the public persona of faith, who gives her life in service to God and the church has trouble keeping the faith, how is she going to preach about it? You are right to be concerned, but I actually think the key to my ability to offer some wisdom on this subject is exactly in the fact that I struggle with it.

First and foremost, the church is in a whole lot of trouble if there is great chasm between the standards we have for our leaders and the standards we have for Christians in general. We are all called to be followers of Christ. We are all called to lead exemplary lives that point to the remarkable life-giving, saving witness of the life, death, and resurrection of our Lord Jesus Christ. And — and this is a very important *and* — we all fall short. No matter who we are, no matter what leadership position we are in, we all fall short. We are human beings. We are fallible. We make mistakes. We hurt those we love and we struggle with our faith. The question is not whether or not we fall short — the question is whether or not we keep striving to be more Christlike in our lives. The question is whether, when we do fall short, we make amends and are humble enough to accept the grace of God when it is offered to us.

I can ultimately speak from a place of strength about the importance of "keeping the faith," but that is because I have struggled with my faith. I have struggled to hold on to my belief in the goodness of God and the possibilities of hope and resurrection in the midst of darkness and loss. I had bone cancer as a young teen. I had eighteen chemotherapy treatments, and each time I was in the worst of it, I would feel horrible. I would have trouble seeing past the next hour. I felt so ill and uncomfortable that I would forget that I ever felt good. I would have trouble keeping the faith that it was going to get better. My vision was so narrowly focused on the present moment that I could not believe that in a few hours I would feel better and in a day or two I would be home and a few days after that I would be back at school. That hope, that possibility, seemed elusive to me, and it was hard to trust in that seemingly far-off reality. But what I could trust in was my mom. As soon as it started to get bad, my mom would say to me, "Remember it is going to get better. I promise, it will get better." Well, I couldn't instantly believe as she did, but I did trust her. That was the first step. I could believe that *she* believed it was going to get better — and that helped.

That was a formative moment for me in my faith life. Because it taught me an essential truth about how we keep the faith. There is a key word we often leave out of the saying "keep the faith." We forget to add "together." That is the thing about keeping the faith, we can only do it together. It took my mom's encouragement, my mom's faith, for me to keep mine. When we try to go it alone, we can fail. We can get lost in our own pain and sadness, our own doubts and challenges. We need community. We need each other. It can be so difficult to keep the faith on our own.

I think that is one of the main purposes of Christian community — we hold the faith for each other. The Christian community does many other noble and important things: we educate each other, we share in fellowship, we do good works in community, we worship, and we celebrate together. But I think the most important thing we do is to hold the faith for each other because that is what keeps us going when we are struggling. And Lord knows, we will all encounter struggles in the course of our lives. We will lose friends and loved ones. We will lose jobs, and dreams will be shattered. We will be traumatized by the violence in our community and the world. We will feel discouraged by the enormity of problems in the world. We will question God. There will be days when we will wonder if the arc of history really does bend toward justice. Those are the days when we need each other, when we need community.

Because the journey from doubt and struggle to faith and hope begins with believing in each other. It begins with believing that the person in the pew next to us has hope — that they believe in the possibility of resurrection and new life, even when we feel surrounded by death and loss. It means trusting in the faith of our family, our friends, our community. It means gathering at this table, together, even when our personal landscape feels rocky and uncertain. It means coming forward to receive the love and grace of God embodied in a wafer and a sip of wine or juice. It means being held up in and by community and knowing somewhere deep inside that we are all held up and all held together by the grace of God.

This is why it matters that we gather together for worship. We can and should pray in our own time by ourselves in the quiet moments and in solitude, but we need community. We need each other. We need to come together for the tangible reminders — in the people gathered, in the prayers we say, in the words from scripture, and in the sacraments we receive — the tangible reminders that we are beloved children of God and that together we can keep the faith.

It is no easy or small thing to "keep the faith," but we can do it. We can do it by diligently reading our Bible so that we learn and remember the stories of how much God loves us and how our brothers and sisters in faith have struggled just as we do. As 2 Timothy 3:16-17 says, "All scripture is inspired by God and is useful for teaching, for reproof, for correction, and for training in righteousness, so that everyone who belongs to God may be proficient, equipped for every good work."

We can keep the faith — together. We can keep the faith by showing up, by gathering together in community to worship God. We need to show up so that we can be held up when we are struggling, and we need to show up so that we can hold others up when we feel confident in our faith. We show up because being in community is an essential part of what it means to be a Christian. I encourage you to keep showing up, because you may never know how your presence might make all the difference in the lives of fellow Christians. It just might be that your showing up today has helped someone start on that journey from doubt to faith. Keep showing up. It matters. Amen.

Proper 25 / Pentecost 23 / Ordinary Time 30
Luke 18:9-14

He also told this parable to some who trusted in themselves that they were righteous and regarded others with contempt: "Two men went up to the temple to pray, one a Pharisee and the other a tax collector. The Pharisee, standing by himself, was praying thus, 'God, I thank you that I am not like other people: thieves, rogues, adulterers, or even like this tax collector. I fast twice a week; I give a tenth of all my income.' But the tax collector, standing far off, would not even look up to heaven, but was beating his breast and saying, 'God, be merciful to me, a sinner!' I tell you, this man went down to his home justified rather than the other; for all who exalt themselves will be humbled, but all who humble themselves will be exalted."

* * *

2 Timothy 4:6-8, 16-18

As for me, I am already being poured out as a libation, and the time of my departure has come. I have fought the good fight, I have finished the race, I have kept the faith. From now on there is reserved for me the crown of righteousness, which the Lord, the righteous judge, will give me on that day, and not only to me but also to all who have longed for his appearing.... At my first defense no one came to my support, but all deserted me. May it not be counted against them! But the Lord stood by me and gave me strength, so that through me the message might be fully proclaimed and all the Gentiles might hear it. So I was rescued from the lion's mouth. The Lord will rescue me from every evil attack and save me for his heavenly kingdom. To him be the glory forever and ever. Amen.

Proper 25 / Pentecost 23 / Ordinary Time 30
Luke 18:9-14
Jeremiah 14:7-10, 19-22; Psalm 84:1-6;
2 Timothy 4:6-8, 16-18

Reflecting God's Abundant Love

May God's Word be spoken. May God's Word be heard. May that point us to the living Word who is Jesus Christ our Lord. Amen.

I lived a portion of my childhood in Bath, Maine. There are many notable things about this small city on the Kennebec River, but it is perhaps best known for its ships. In the late 1800s and early 1900s it was full of shipyards that built all kinds of wooden sailing vessels. Now it has just one shipyard, Bath Iron Works, which is a huge facility that builds destroyers and frigates for the US Navy. Much of the work is done outside, and it was great fun to watch the pieces of the ship come together like a giant puzzle. Thousands of people work at Bath Iron Works in three shifts around the clock. In fact, after the state government BIW is the largest employer in the state of Maine. The difference from the state offices is that almost all the BIW employees work in Bath, and there is really only one major road in and out of town. This meant that the schedules of everyone in town were arranged around the shift changes. You generally didn't want to be anywhere near the gates of the yard at 3:30 in the afternoon because of the flood of people and cars. You could wait a while. The bottleneck of traffic was at its worst at the on-ramp to Route 1 and the bridge over the Kennebec River. When I was a child it was only a two-lane bridge, so everyone coming from BIW and town had to merge with the traffic already on the bridge to go north. Mainers generally pride themselves on being a friendly bunch, and it was interesting to note what happened when the traffic from BIW joined the bridge. Very quickly a civilized system of alternating would emerge. A car on the bridge would go, then one from the ramp, then one from the bridge, and so on. It was as though everyone had just agreed that this was in everyone's best interest. It was. It kept the traffic moving. No one got aggravated and everyone got where they were going in a reasonable amount of time.

But in the summer months when the traffic volume increased with all the visiting tourists — many of whom didn't hold to the belief "wouldn't it be nice if we just alternated?" — competition reigned, horns blared, and the traffic would be backed up for miles at 3:30 in the afternoon. Some of this was just due to an increase in the sheer volume of cars on the road, but I can't help to think it still would have gone better if everyone had just taken a deep breath and alternated. In fact, I often think about that tidy, kind system whenever I am in merging traffic. Wouldn't this all go better if we just alternated? Why do we get so stressed out and turn it into a competition over who gets there ten seconds sooner?

I think the kingdom of God is meant to be one of cooperation and understanding. I don't think competition and greed or self-centeredness are supposed to be our governing principles. I think the kingdom of God looks more like everyone taking turns and being friendly than a place of blaring horns and frustration. I don't think our faith life is meant to be a competition. Why then does it so often feel like one?

We have scripture passages like the epistle from 2 Timothy 4:7-8: "I have fought the good fight, I have finished the race, I have kept the faith. From now on there is reserved for me the crown of righteousness, which the Lord, the righteous judge, will give me on that day, and not only to me but also to all who have longed for his appearing." If it is a race and a fight at the end of which we receive a crown, it can be very easy to believe that our life as Christians is meant to be a competition. Races and crowns make it sound much more like the World Cup or Formula One than some cooperative, friendly endeavor.

If we read 2 Timothy as making it about a competition *with each other* then I think we are mistaken. The fight and the race discussed there were not against fellow Christians, they were against the forces of evil. We do have to fight as Christians. We have to fight against all the forces in this world, all the temptations that lead us away from following Jesus. That is the important fight — and it is real. A quick glance at a few television advertisements or a few magazine covers will easily remind us that the world is full of temptations to spend more, be lazy, be gluttonous, choose brief enjoyment over taking care of ourselves. A brief glance at the news headlines is all we need to remind ourselves that evil is real and at work in the world. There are far too many people who see violence and terror as the only way to advance their own selfish agendas.

I am not sure a simple reinterpretation of 2 Timothy is all it would take to keep us from being competitive with each other. I wish it were! But it turns out we are human and competition seems to be a natural part of who we are. We seem to believe that there is not enough love or wealth or praise in this world to go around. We feel we must be in competition with each other for anything good. This is one of the reasons why I love today's gospel passage. "Two men went up to the temple to pray, one a Pharisee and the other a tax collector. The Pharisee, standing by himself, was praying thus, 'God, I thank you that I am not like other people: thieves, rogues, adulterers, or even like this tax collector. I fast twice a week; I give a tenth of all my income.' The tax collector, standing far off, would not even look up to heaven, but was beating his breast and saying, 'God, be merciful to me, a sinner!' I tell you, this man went down to his home justified rather than the other; for all who exalt themselves will be humbled, but all who humble themselves will be exalted" (Luke 18:10-14). I love this passage because it describes humanity so well!

We all like to think we are like the tax collector, willing to admit when we have gone astray, humble and contrite, seeking mercy for our sins. Hopefully most of the time we are like the tax collector, a paragon of humility, seeking only to follow the Lord and do right. Three cheers and a pat on the back for all the times we have been like the tax collector!

But what about the times we are like the Pharisee? What about the times in which we are guilty of comparing ourselves to others? What about the times in which we fall prey to believing that life is a competition, and we must do better than those around us? It is much harder to admit the times when we have gotten on our high horses and been self-centered like the Pharisee. It is harder to admit how much time we spend comparing ourselves to our neighbors. Who has a nicer car or a nicer house? Who has lost weight or gained weight? Who gives more or less than we do? Whose church has more people or more going on? Which cities have more or fewer problems than we do? We all do it. That is why this gospel story is so true, because the Pharisee perfectly encapsulates the human experience. We have all had our moments of comparing ourselves to others, of trying to figure out how it is that we are better or worse off in any number of categories than those around us. We all have our Pharisee moments. The difficulty is not in having Pharisee moments, the difficulty is when we let the Pharisee's beliefs become our foundational beliefs. The difficulty is when we allow our desire for attention and to be "the best" to get the better of us. We may begin to believe that life really is a competition. When we make our decisions based on what will make ourselves look good rather than what is best for all involved, we fail.

The biggest issue here is what the Pharisee's belief says about God. If what the Pharisee says is true, then God is capricious and vain. The Pharisee's view is a theology of scarcity. It promotes the belief that God would not or cannot love both a Pharisee and a tax collector; that God somehow loves us more when we are superior to our neighbors. No, that is not our God. Our God is a God of abundance and authenticity. Our God is a God who loves each and every one of us — for we are his beloved children. God's love for us is not based on our appearance or our mere acts of piety. God cares about what is in our hearts. God cares that we are grounded in love and not motivated by a selfish desire to do more or have more, but by a love of neighbor that seeks to promote the flourishing of all God's children.

We as Christians are called to ground our lives in love: love of God, love of neighbor, love of self. We are called to be co-creators with God, to participate in building the kingdom of God. We are called to a kingdom built on trust, cooperation, and sharing — not a kingdom based on competition or a theology of scarcity. While we have our moments of being like the Pharisee, and while our world is full of temptations to go astray, it is also a world that is full of abundant blessings. Our perception makes all the difference. If we look for the blessings, if we look for the acts grounded in love, we will find them.

That is our choice today. Are we going to be a people of scarcity, competing with each other to impress God? Or are we going to be a people of abundance? Are we going to be people who feel in their hearts the deep, abiding, abundant love of God? Can we be a people who go out and share that love in the world?

There is our choice: competition or love? Let us choose love. God always does. Amen.

Proper 26 / Pentecost 24 / Ordinary Time 31
Luke 19:1-10

He entered Jericho and was passing through it. A man was there named Zacchaeus; he was a chief tax collector and was rich. He was trying to see who Jesus was, but on account of the crowd he could not, because he was short in stature. So he ran ahead and climbed a sycamore tree to see him, because he was going to pass that way. When Jesus came to the place, he looked up and said to him, "Zacchaeus, hurry and come down; for I must stay at your house today." So he hurried down and was happy to welcome him. All who saw it began to grumble and said, "He has gone to be the guest of one who is a sinner." Zacchaeus stood there and said to the Lord, "Look, half of my possessions, Lord, I will give to the poor; and if I have defrauded anyone of anything, I will pay back four times as much." Then Jesus said to him, "Today salvation has come to this house, because he too is a son of Abraham. For the Son of Man came to seek out and to save the lost."

* * *

2 Thessalonians 1:1-4, 11-12

Paul, Silvanus, and Timothy, To the church of the Thessalonians in God our Father and the Lord Jesus Christ: Grace to you and peace from God our Father and the Lord Jesus Christ. We must always give thanks to God for you, brothers and sisters, as is right, because your faith is growing abundantly, and the love of everyone of you for one another is increasing. Therefore we ourselves boast of you among the churches of God for your steadfastness and faith during all your persecutions and the afflictions that you are enduring.... To this end we always pray for you, asking that our God will make you worthy of his call and will fulfill by his power every good resolve and work of faith, so that the name of our Lord Jesus may be glorified in you, and you in him, according to the grace of our God and the Lord Jesus Christ.

Proper 26 / Pentecost 24 / Ordinary Time 31
Luke 19:1-10
2 Thessalonians 1:1-4, 11-12

Making a Difference

My college friend Amelia is well-off by any standard. Her parents hired a circus for her fifth birthday party. Her mother has china and place settings for 100 people. Her father is a doctor who made a breakthrough discovery that helped millions and made a fortune for his family. There are libraries named after him on multiple college campuses.

On the surface, she might seem to be just like Zacchaeus. One of the 1% who has been aloof to the needs and concerns of the other 99%.

In our gospel today, we hear of Jesus' encounter with the rich tax collector, Zacchaeus. At first we all think we know where this story is going. We know what Jesus thought of the rich. He so often spoke critically or disparagingly of them. We might be expecting Jesus to be critical of Zacchaeus, to chide him for the wealth he has amassed. Remember how he chided the rich man who did not wish to give up his possessions to inherit eternal life? Think of the parable of Lazarus and the rich man that shows us the perils of ignoring those around us who are in need.

But the next sentence in our reading for today gives us a clue that this story might not just be a story about criticizing the wealthy. As we read on, we realize that Zacchaeus was looking for Jesus. Zacchaeus was not just your average rich man who was content as he was. He had heard about Jesus. What we see in Zacchaeus is the stirring of the Holy Spirit and the desire to do things differently. Jesus recognized this stirring in Zacchaeus and went to his house. As usual, the fact that Jesus broke the rules and went to eat with someone who was not well liked by society upset the crowd. Zacchaeus was, after all, a tax collector who had made his money on the backs of his own people. He was not well liked by those around him. Perhaps they were jealous — who wouldn't want Jesus to come for dinner? Of course, they did not recognize what Jesus was beginning to recognize — that Zacchaeus was about to make a change in his life.

Amazingly we get to that transformation rather quickly, for Zacchaeus immediately makes a promise: "Look, half of my possessions, Lord, I will give to the poor; and if I have defrauded anyone of anything, I will pay back four times as much" (v. 8). Zacchaeus was transforming his life. He was not going to be a rich man who hoarded what he had or ignored the needs of those around him. He was a rich man who was going to be a model of humility and generosity.

Just like Zacchaeus, my friend Amelia is not what she might seem on the surface. While she was born into wealth, there were times when she had to go without. Her parents divorced when she was a teenager, and sadly it was a long and bitter divorce. For a time all her mother's assets were frozen and she and her mother were locked out of their house. Amelia and her mother spent months in a Howard Johnson's motel room living as cheaply as they could, for they had no idea how long it would be before they could go home again. Thankfully things were resolved, Amelia was given a wonderful education, and she has personal financial security.

The gift that Amelia has given me is an example of what it means to live faithfully with the resources we have been given. While Amelia has again been blessed with an abundance of financial resources, she has never forgotten what it was like to be without. Just as Zacchaeus came to realize, for Amelia wealth is a gift to be shared. She has always been generous with her money and used it to help others. What has inspired me in Amelia's attitude is that she sees her money as a means and not an end. She knows it is a gift and a fragile one. She well knows that in an instant it can all be gone. She does not worship her money or try to hoard it. She sees it as a means to a full life — the means for education and travel for herself and her family. It is the means to enrichment in her own life and for her community. I think this is what Jesus was really getting at in the gospel today.

The transformation Zacchaeus comes to is what Amelia learned long ago — possessions do not last; they are not eternal. God is. We need to put our faith in God. We need to live a life that first and foremost is focused on love of God and love of neighbor. Whatever assets we may have, however much money is in our bank accounts is secondary. Financial wealth is a gift, and one that may not last.

Just because we don't make money our first priority that doesn't mean money doesn't matter. It matters a great deal. It enables us to have food and shelter, to get an education, to travel, and to have fun experiences with our families. All of these things matter, for they enrich our lives and provide enjoyment. God desires us to have life and have it abundantly. God definitely is in favor of our having fun! And as Jesus rewarded Zacchaeus for his transformation, for his decision to share what he had and to make a difference in the world, so he calls each of us to do the same. He calls us to see our wealth as a means to make a difference in the world.

Whether you feel financially strapped or financially comfortable at the moment, I ask you to reflect on the place money has in your life. If it has an overwhelming influence or an uncomfortably central place in your life, I ask you to consider a change of heart. What would it look like to see money only as a means? How can you, like Zacchaeus and Amelia, let go of the hold money has in your life? How can you use whatever assets you have to enrich your life and the lives of others? Money may not be permanent, but we can use it make a lasting difference in the lives of others. The question I leave you with today is this: How is your money making a difference in the world? Amen.

Proper 27 / Pentecost 25 / Ordinary Time 32
Luke 20:27-38

Some Sadducees, those who say there is no resurrection, came to him and asked him a question, "Teacher, Moses wrote for us that if a man's brother dies, leaving a wife but no children, the man shall marry the widow and raise up children for his brother. Now there were seven brothers; the first married, and died childless; then the second and the third married her, and so in the same way all seven died childless. Finally the woman also died. In the resurrection, therefore, whose wife will the woman be? For the seven had married her." Jesus said to them, "Those who belong to this age marry and are given in marriage; but those who are considered worthy of a place in that age and in the resurrection from the dead neither marry nor are given in marriage. Indeed they cannot die anymore, because they are like angels and are children of God, being children of the resurrection. And the fact that the dead are raised Moses himself showed, in the story about the bush, where he speaks of the Lord as the God of Abraham, the God of Isaac, and the God of Jacob. Now he is God not of the dead, but of the living; for to him all of them are alive."

* * *

2 Thessalonians 2:1-5, 13-17

As to the coming of our Lord Jesus Christ and our being gathered together to him, we beg you, brothers and sisters, not to be quickly shaken in mind or alarmed, either by spirit or by word or by letter, as though from us, to the effect that the day of the Lord is already here. Let no one deceive you in any way; for that day will not come unless the rebellion comes first and the lawless one is revealed, the one destined for destruction. He opposes and exalts himself above every so-called god or object of worship, so that he takes his seat in the temple of God, declaring himself to be God. Do you not remember that I told you these things when I was still with you? ... But we must always give thanks to God for you, brothers and sisters beloved by the Lord, because God chose you as the firstfruits for salvation through sanctification by the Spirit and through belief in the truth. For this purpose he called you through our proclamation of the good news, so that you may obtain the glory of our Lord Jesus Christ. So then, brothers and sisters, stand firm and hold fast to the traditions that you were taught by us, either by word of mouth or by our letter. Now may our Lord Jesus Christ himself and God our Father, who loved us and through grace gave us eternal comfort and good hope, comfort your hearts and strengthen them in every good work and word.

Proper 27 / Pentecost 25 / Ordinary Time 32
Luke 20:27-38
Job 19:23-27a; Psalm 17:1-9;
2 Thessalonians 2:1-5, 13-17

Thy Will Be Done

Recently, I was in a bit of a hurry to get something done (which I am slowly discovering is rarely a good idea). I was moving things around at home, and I broke the lamp in my husband's study. I felt badly about what I had done, and I wanted to remedy the situation. I offered to go right out and buy him a new lamp. He said not to worry; it wasn't his favorite lamp anyway, and we could go and get a lamp later in the week. There was no rush. This is where we do not see eye-to-eye. My husband is very patient and careful about the purchases he makes. He would rather sit in the dark for a few days and be sure to find just the right lamp than rush right out and get the wrong one. I, on the other hand, am a problem-solver who likes to find an immediate solution. I love to fix things quickly, and in my drive to fix things, I will often opt for any solution, so that the problem can be fixed. But often times, as with the lamp, my quick fix is not the *right* solution to the problem.

So if we apply today's gospel lesson to this little incident, I was behaving like a Sadducee. I was stuck in my own frame of reference, and I needed to be reminded of the bigger picture. I needed to be reminded that *my* answer is not necessarily the right one. The Sadducees went up to Jesus and asked him this long and complicated question about how a particular Jewish law regarding marriage might be applicable in the afterlife. The Sadducees did not believe in the resurrection, and they were hoping to trick Jesus with this question. They were hoping to undermine his teaching and authority. Jesus did not let this happen. He affirmed the reality of the resurrection and showed the Sadducees the error of their ways. He showed them that they were trying to apply categories that belong to our human, finite life to the afterlife, to that which is infinite and beyond our full comprehension. He showed them that resurrected life will not be the same as human life, so it is wrong to apply the same categories to it. Jesus is asking them to broaden their vision and to change their perspective. But the Sadducees are stuck in their own world and cannot broaden their vision.

It is so easy to get stuck in our own little worlds. We keep our vision focused on ourselves or on what is immediately around us. It is easy to assume that we know what the right answer is or what the right thing to do is in a given situation. It is easy to assume that our experience is the same as others'. I assumed my husband would want a quick solution to the lamp problem because I did. I must remember that what holds true for myself is not necessarily true for others.

This is what the gospel lesson is showing us. It is reminding us of the ways in which we can behave like the Sadducees. Just as they needed a reminder, so do we. We need a reminder to broaden our vision — a reminder to change our perspective. We need a reminder that our calling as Christians is not to follow our own desires or our own categories — it is to follow God's will. Every time we say the Lord's Prayer, we pray, "Our Father who art in heaven, hallowed be thy name, thy will be done." We do not pray "*my* will be done." Being a follower of Christ means that we commit to imitating Christ. We commit to following his model of self-giving. We acknowledge that God comes first, not our own selfish desires. We imitate him who gave himself over to God's will.

Think of Christ's prayer in the Garden of Gethsemane. "My Father, if it be possible, let this cup pass from me;

nevertheless, not as I will, but as you will" (Matthew 26:39). Christ prays first that the cup be taken from him. This is the part we can most relate to in a very human way; Jesus acknowledges that he does not wish to face the pain and suffering he knows is coming. Yet the prayer does not end there. He goes on to pray that God's will be done, not his own. Ultimately, he gives himself over as a servant of God's will.

This may seem like an extraordinary act of self-sacrifice that we could not possibly be capable of, but in fact it is probably one we do on an almost daily basis. We just might not see it that way. Think of a beloved person in your life, a spouse, a child, a parent, a friend. Think of all the ways in which you give up something of yourself — your time, your resources, your love, because you know it makes a difference in their well-being. It is easy to give of yourself because you know the joy it brings you to see that beloved person happy and well. We all know of stories from 9/11 or natural disasters where people were willing to sacrifice themselves for complete strangers. If we are willing to sacrifice for those we love, and even those we don't know, why would we not be willing to do it for God? Why would we not give ourselves over to God's will? Perhaps it is because we often keep our focus narrow. Like the first part of Jesus' prayer, all we see is the pain of Jesus' trial and crucifixion. But if we broaden our perspective and look at the big picture, all of a sudden things look a little different. We see Easter morning. We see an empty tomb. We see resurrection.

So, we are reminded that when we narrow our focus, we cut ourselves off from possibilities. We cut ourselves off from the big picture. It is incumbent upon us as Christians to remember that the big picture is a picture of resurrection. It is a picture of hope. We are not to impose our categories on God nor on other people. To do so is arrogant, but it can also be self-destructive. Racing out to buy my spouse a new lamp might have made me feel better in the short term, but in the end it would not have contributed to our happiness. It is when we slow down, when we turn ourselves over to God, acknowledging that we do not have the right answer, and we are seeking God's joy as we seek the joy of those we love, that our vision expands and new and marvelous possibilities emerge.

In his response to the Sadducees, Christ affirmed the reality of resurrection. He affirmed God's desire for life, abundant life for all people. That life-giving reality can be affirmed on a daily basis in our own lives, if we are open to the possibility, and if we live out our prayer, "Thy will be done." Amen.

Proper 28 / Pentecost 26 / Ordinary Time 33
Luke 21:5-19

When some were speaking about the temple, how it was adorned with beautiful stones and gifts dedicated to God, he said, "As for these things that you see, the days will come when not one stone will be left upon another; all will be thrown down." They asked him, "Teacher, when will this be, and what will be the sign that this is about to take place?" And he said, "Beware that you are not led astray; for many will come in my name and say, 'I am he!' and, 'The time is near!' Do not go after them. When you hear of wars and insurrections, do not be terrified; for these things must take place first, but the end will not follow immediately." Then he said to them, "Nation will rise against nation, and kingdom against kingdom; there will be great earthquakes, and in various places famines and plagues; and there will be dreadful portents and great signs from heaven. But before all this occurs, they will arrest you and persecute you; they will hand you over to synagogues and prisons, and you will be brought before kings and governors because of my name. This will give you an opportunity to testify. So make up your minds not to prepare your defense in advance; for I will give you words and a wisdom that none of your opponents will be able to withstand or contradict. You will be betrayed even by parents and brothers, by relatives and friends; and they will put some of you to death. You will be hated by all because of my name. But not a hair of your head will perish. By your endurance you will gain your souls."

* * *

2 Thessalonians 3:6-13

Now we command you, beloved, in the name of our Lord Jesus Christ, to keep away from believers who are living in idleness and not according to the tradition that they received from us. For you yourselves know how you ought to imitate us; we were not idle when we were with you, and we did not eat anyone's bread without paying for it; but with toil and labor we worked night and day, so that we might not burden any of you. This was not because we do not have that right, but in order to give you an example to imitate. For even when we were with you, we gave you this command: Anyone unwilling to work should not eat. For we hear that some of you are living in idleness, mere busybodies, not doing any work. Now such persons we command and exhort in the Lord Jesus Christ to do their work quietly and to earn their own living. Brothers and sisters, do not be weary in doing what is right.

Proper 28 / Pentecost 26 / Ordinary Time 33
Luke 21:5-19
2 Thessalonians 3:6-13

The Time Is Near

"And he said, 'Beware that you are not led astray; for many will come in my name and say, "I am he!" and, "The time is near!" Do not go after them'" (v. 8). This is the heart of our gospel reading today. For those of us who live a comfortable middle class existence, it can be easy to dismiss our whole reading with its predictions of persecutions, earthquakes, and famines. How could those apply to our lives? For those of us who live comfortable lives in Christian majority countries, we do not know what it is to be persecuted for our faith. And if we live a comfortable middle-class existence, we likely have never really been hungry, so we cannot even begin to imagine what it is like to go for a long period of time without enough to eat. Depending on where we live, an earthquake might be a real possibility, but we likely live in a well-designed house and operate in a community with an early warning system. So "earthquake" does not mean the same thing for us that it did for our ancestors.

This seems a text designed for its original hearers. It seems designed for the early Christians for whom the end of the world and the return of Christ seemed imminent. Those who did not have scientific or economic explanations for famines or earthquakes; those who lived in a world where choosing to follow Jesus and acknowledge him as the Messiah, as the Son of God, was to take your life in your hands — quite literally. For thousands in the early years of the church, being a Christian meant persecution and frequently death. So how could this gospel text about the end times and the likelihood of persecution be relevant to us in the twenty-first century?

Here I return to Jesus' command: "Beware that you are not led astray; for many will come in my name and say, 'I am he!' and, 'The time is near!' Do not go after them." Beware that you are not led astray. There is a message to which we twenty-first-century Christians can relate. While we may not face the same immediate life and death situations as so many of our forebearers in the faith did, we do face considerable temptations. We are, in fact, in great danger of being led astray.

The temptations in this world are great. Many of us may be confronted by those who demean our faith and point out all that is wrong with institutional religion. They often seem content in their beliefs and can tempt us to think our lives would be easier if we just gave up on this whole following Jesus thing.

Every day we are bombarded by advertisements that tell us that if only we drank this coffee or drove this car or banked at this bank our lives would be the picture of fulfillment. We are surrounded by clever and creative enticements to buy more, to buy into the idea that material goods can give our lives meaning, and make us feel fulfilled. And it is all too tempting to give in to our own selfish desires. When we are wronged, it is tempting to give into a desire for revenge or vengeance. When we are angry, it is tempting to lash out in anger and to hurt those we love. It is tempting to give in to our own laziness — to stay in bed instead of going to church, to postpone giving more to those in need, being a more active member of our community, and the like, until next year or when it is more convenient for us.

That is not who Jesus asks us to be. That is not the life he calls us to. He does not call us to laziness, material gluttony, or to a faith that cherry-picks the simple and fun parts. No, Jesus calls us to be his followers, to be Christians. Jesus calls us to engage deeply with our faith and to be committed. We are called to be committed to living lives of faithful discipleship. This does not mean that our lives will be easy. There have been and no doubt will be times when we want to give in to temptation. When we want to seek immediate gratification or the path that seems easier, but we would be wrong to do so.

This is not just a matter of blindly following a leader because he asked us to follow. The path of being a Christian may be challenging at times, and it may not always seem like the easy road, but it is a path worth following for our reward is great. I know what you may be thinking — not this "your reward is in heaven" stuff again. The church has tried that before and it didn't go well. Well, don't worry, I am not implying that we should spend our earthly lives suffering so we can seek a reward in heaven. I firmly believe there are rewards for our faith lives right here and now.

Being a follower of Jesus satisfies a hunger and a desire in my soul — a desire for meaning and acceptance. Being a follower of Jesus means that I am not alone in this. Even on the bad days when I feel unworthy or as though I am carrying the weight of the world, I am not alone. God is with me and even when I feel uncertain about the future or my place in it, I know that it is not all about me. I can trust that I am a part of something much bigger than me. I can trust that in some small way, I do matter. I am a beloved child of God, and in some way my being present — *each* of us being present on this earth matters. We are a part of something big. We are a part of building the kingdom of God, a part of making the world a better place.

While the personal, internal, and spiritual reward of following Jesus is significant, I believe it also matters because following Jesus inspires us to be our best and to do our best in the world. Following Jesus inspires us to be better people, to pay attention to the needs of those around us, to do our part to make this broken, sinful world a bit more like the kingdom of God.

May we commit ourselves to following Jesus more deeply. May we commit ourselves to resisting the myriad of temptations that distract us from his way. May we commit ourselves to sharing the good news and doing our part to build up the kingdom. Amen.

Christ the King Sunday
Proper 29 / Pentecost 27 / Ordinary Time 34
Luke 23:33-43

When they came to the place that is called The Skull, they crucified Jesus there with the criminals, one on his right and one on his left. Then Jesus said, "Father, forgive them; for they do not know what they are doing." And they cast lots to divide his clothing. And the people stood by, watching; but the leaders scoffed at him, saying, "He saved others; let him save himself if he is the Messiah of God, his chosen one!" The soldiers also mocked him, coming up and offering him sour wine, and saying, "If you are the King of the Jews, save yourself!" There was also an inscription over him, "This is the King of the Jews." One of the criminals who were hanged there kept deriding him and saying, "Are you not the Messiah? Save yourself and us!" But the other rebuked him, saying, "Do you not fear God, since you are under the same sentence of condemnation? And we indeed have been condemned justly, for we are getting what we deserve for our deeds, but this man has done nothing wrong." Then he said, "Jesus, remember me when you come into your kingdom." He replied, "Truly I tell you, today you will be with me in Paradise."

* * *

Colossians 1:11-20

May you be made strong with all the strength that comes from his glorious power, and may you be prepared to endure everything with patience, while joyfully giving thanks to the Father, who has enabled you to share in the inheritance of the saints in the light. He has rescued us from the power of darkness and transferred us into the kingdom of his beloved

Son, in whom we have redemption, the forgiveness of sins. He is the image of the invisible God, the firstborn of all creation; for in him all things in heaven and on earth were created, things visible and invisible, whether thrones or dominions or rulers or powers — all things have been created through him and for him. He himself is before all things, and in him all things hold together. He is the head of the body, the church; he is the beginning, the firstborn from the dead, so that he might come to have first place in everything. For in him all the fullness of God was pleased to dwell, and through him God was pleased to reconcile to himself all things, whether on earth or in heaven, by making peace through the blood of his cross.

Christ the King Sunday
Proper 29 / Pentecost 27 / Ordinary Time 34
Luke 23:33-43
Jeremiah 23:1-6; Psalm 46; Colossians 1:11-20

Christ's Monarchy

Today is Christ the King Sunday. Our readings — particularly those from Colossians and Luke's gospel — are all offering us images of Christ as our king. Like any good American, I have mixed feelings about monarchy. There is a romanticism about the monarchy. I love the stories of princes and princesses, kings and queens. While those make nice stories, when it comes down to it, I will also admit to a patriotism that can tend to a bit of self-aggrandizement. Remarkably, for over two centuries we have managed a peaceful transfer of power every few years between civilians who were frequently at opposite ends of the political spectrum. The liberty and freedoms we all enjoy, the fact that so many still seek to emigrate to this country, are a testament to the tremendous benefits of our democratic government. We do have a government by the people and for the people. I love that each of our votes count, and we get to have a say in our government. History has certainly shown us that when all the power is in the hands of a single person, tragedy results. Think of Hitler and Mussolini or any of the numerous dictatorships in Africa and South America in recent decades. Millions died and bloody wars were often required to bring a return of peace and stability.

But does it always have to be that way? I am not sure that it does. I have to say that as a parent a more totalitarian regime is appealing. If we allowed the egalitarian democracy of American society to rule in our house, we would probably be eating macaroni and cheese on an almost daily basis and *Thomas the Train* would be repeating on our DVD player. Not to mention that the entire contents of the toy cupboard would take up permanent residence on our living room floor. There is something to be said for the fact that parents know better than kids what is good for them. It would be risky and downright dangerous to allow children to literally govern themselves. A visit to any Juvenile Detention Center would remind us that if some kids are not taught the difference between right and wrong, if they are not given structure and self-esteem, they are capable of terribly destructive behavior. And there are other institutions like the military, where a more dictatorial form of governance works well. In the military following orders can often mean the difference between life and death. In many cases we need structure and strong governance.

Humans do not seem to be able to govern ourselves perfectly. Even our American democracy works because it isn't pure democracy. Power is not equally shared among all the people. We choose to invest the majority of power in three branches of government with checks and balances. We have a system designed to safeguard against individual temptations or tendencies to sin. We spread the power out so that no one can monopolize it.

This balanced form of government, with all the rights and freedoms it provides, can make us a bit skeptical of all the talk of monarchy in our readings today. Do we really want a leader who is lord over all of us? Might we prefer our readings to talk of a "democratically elected president" rather than a "king"? We might. But I think it is worth noting how different a king Jesus is than any of the human examples we have.

This is where the parenting image can help. A system of governance that trends toward the totalitarian works in a family because there is a vast knowledge gap between parents and children. Parents know what is best — their vision and understanding is much broader and more far-reaching than that of a child. They know that good things will come of eating broccoli and cleaning up one's room no matter how distasteful these actions may be for the child at the present moment.

The parenting image can be problematic, however, for we all sadly know stories of parents who abused their power, whose totalitarian tendencies resulted in physical and emotional scars that their children bore for the rest of their lives. Again we have to remind ourselves that Christ is not like us. His kingship is not subject to the worst of human tendencies. It only has the best of what humanity has to offer. Christ does not fall into temptation and sin as we do. Christ is the perfect parent. His vision is so much bigger and broader than ours. He knows what we need before we do. He has our best interests at heart and is seeking to help us to mature into the beautiful, gifted people he has called us to be.

In a true monarchy, subjects are required to swear an oath of faithfulness and obedience to the king. We do this too — we do it in the vows we say (or our parents and godparents say on our behalf) at baptism. We promise to follow Christ as our Lord and Savior — repenting and returning to that path whenever we fall into sin. We promise to do good works, to worship, and to pray. We promise to respect the dignity of all and to strive to make the world a better place — to transform this earthly world into a kingdom that better reflects the kingship of Christ.

Just as in a monarchy, Christ asks us to give our all, to be faithful and obedient. While we may be tempted by the allure of worldly power or the desire for self-control, we are called to trust. We are called to trust in Christ as our Lord and Savior. We are called to turn our lives over and give ourselves to the building up of God's kingdom. If all that we believe about God is true — and I believe it is — and that Christ is the loving and merciful Lord he has shown himself to be, then there is nothing lost in turning our lives over. In fact, if we can have the courage to let go and give ourselves to God's guidance, our lives are only bound to be more blessed than they already are. Amen.

Reformation Day
John 8:31-36

Then Jesus said to the Jews who had believed in him, "If you continue in my word, you are truly my disciples; and you will know the truth, and the truth will make you free." They answered him, "We are descendants of Abraham and have never been slaves to anyone. What do you mean by saying, 'You will be made free'?" Jesus answered them, "Very truly, I tell you, everyone who commits sin is a slave to sin. The slave does not have a permanent place in the household; the son has a place there forever. So if the Son makes you free, you will be free indeed."

* * *

Romans 3:19-28

Now we know that whatever the law says, it speaks to those who are under the law, so that every mouth may be silenced, and the whole world may be held accountable to God. For "no human being will be justified in his sight" by deeds prescribed by the law, for through the law comes the knowledge of sin. But now, apart from law, the righteousness of God has been disclosed, and is attested by the law and the prophets, the righteousness of God through faith in Jesus Christ for all who believe. For there is no distinction, since all have sinned and fall short of the glory of God; they are now justified by his grace as a gift, through the redemption that is in Christ Jesus, whom God put forward as a sacrifice of atonement by his blood, effective through faith. He did this to show his righteousness, because in his divine forbearance he had passed over the sins previously committed; it was to prove at the present time that he himself is righteous and that he justifies the one who has faith in Jesus. Then what becomes of boasting? It is excluded. By what law? By that of works? No, but by the law of faith. For we hold that a person is justified by faith apart from works prescribed by the law.

Reformation Day
John 8:31-36
Jeremiah 31:31-34; Psalm 46; Romans 3:19-28

The Definition of Church

I grew up in small town in Maine. So small that the Episcopal church in town, St. John's, was just a historic building used for events and concerts. It wasn't an active parish. We worshiped in the next town over which was big enough to have a real downtown and a wonderful Episcopal parish, St. Philip's. I loved that community for the ways in which it supported and formed me, and for the valuable lessons it taught me. One of those lessons was about what it means to be a church. They taught me that being a church is about people and community. It is *not* about the building. St. John's in my town was a beautiful, historic building, but it wasn't a church because there weren't any people there. Its doors were rarely open. No one gathered there for prayer or worship. People weren't fed there. The powerful, amazing message of God's reconciling love was not proclaimed there by word or deed. Most of the time it was just an empty building.

St. Philip's, on the other hand, was a community that worshiped God in word, prayer, and deed. They fed the needy from their food pantry, celebrated the bounty of God's creation with an annual Strawberry Festival, and ladled countless bowls of fish chowder to tourists and locals alike each summer. It was a vibrant place that taught me that church is about community and people. This message was brought home to me each summer and winter. Each summer we would have at least one Sunday where we held church outside — at a local farm or on the shores of a lake. And for many winters, when money was tight and the parish struggled to pay the heating bills, they would close up the church and move into the parish hall. But no matter where we were, it was still church. Little children still ran around and tugged on the priest's rope belt during the service. Passing the peace still took ten minutes because we loved to greet each other. God was worshiped and all the ministries of the parish still happened. Our sense of community came from who was gathered; not from where we were gathered or what stuff we had.

As the saying goes, "The most important things in life are not things." And this is exactly the message God has for us today in the reading from Jeremiah. The Israelites had been given the sign of God's covenant with them in the form of stone tablets, and those had broken. The Israelites, like all of us, were forever falling into the temptation of worshiping local idols. There is the famous golden calf incident, where they got tired of waiting for Moses to come down from the mountain, and so they melted their jewelry into a golden calf and decided to worship it instead of God. They lost their focus and got caught up in the temptation of the material world. The Israelites thought they had the problem all sorted out when they built the temple in Jerusalem. The put the Ark of the Covenant there and thought they had solved the problem by providing a physical place to worship God. Then Jerusalem was invaded, the temple was destroyed, and the people were exiled. We then get the important lesson from Jeremiah.

God said, "I will put my law within them, and I will write it on their hearts; and I will be their God, and they shall be my people." The Israelites learned that their identity as beloved children of God was not attached to any material entity — it was not about how much money they had or how nice a temple they built for God. Their connection to God was written not on any stone tablet that could be destroyed by an invading army — it was written on their hearts. They may not have had their temple or their tablets anymore, but that didn't mean they could not worship or praise God. God was with them wherever they were. The community of the Israelites learned to worship God wherever they were — in homes or in public places. They defined a worshiping community not by where they were, but by whether or not two people were present.

This is a reminder I need often. In my personal life, I can easily get too focused on the material world. I too am swayed by advertisers to think that my life will be vastly improved if I just buy this gadget or that new toy. But the substance of life is not in the things I have. The substance of life is in the relationships I build. The substance of life is in the community gathered in prayer and in participation in God's mission. That is where the beauty and the meaning are.

This is a reminder we all need to hear as Christians. The church is filled with wonderful, vibrant, worshiping communities — people who are gathered together to pray and to share God's reconciling love in countless ministries in their communities. The trouble is that many of these communities are also drowning under the cost of caring for buildings that are no longer appropriate for the needs of the community. These are beautiful buildings with tremendous history and sentimental value, but if we cannot sustain them, we need to hear this important message from Jeremiah. We need to remember that a church is defined by the people and not by the building.

It is my prayer that we will find ways to celebrate the communities we are — to celebrate the ways in which we are bound together by love of God and love of neighbor — and to let go of those material things that prevent us from living into the fullness of our identity as God's beloved children who are called to share God's reconciling love with the world. Amen.

All Saints Day
Luke 6:20-31

Then he looked up at his disciples and said: "Blessed are you who are poor, for yours is the kingdom of God. Blessed are you who are hungry now, for you will be filled. Blessed are you who weep now, for you will laugh. Blessed are you when people hate you, and when they exclude you, revile you, and defame you on account of the Son of Man. Rejoice in that day and leap for joy, for surely your reward is great in heaven; for that is what their ancestors did to the prophets. But woe to you who are rich, for you have received your consolation. Woe to you who are full now, for you will be hungry. Woe to you who are laughing now, for you will mourn and weep. Woe to you when all speak well of you, for that is what their ancestors did to the false prophets. But I say to you that listen, Love your enemies, do good to those who hate you, bless those who curse you, pray for those who abuse you. If anyone strikes you on the cheek, offer the other also; and from anyone who takes away your coat do not withhold even your shirt. Give to everyone who begs from you; and if anyone takes away your goods, do not ask for them again. Do to others as you would have them do to you."

* * *

Ephesians 1:11-23

In Christ we have also obtained an inheritance, having been destined according to the purpose of him who accomplishes all things according to his counsel and will, so that we, who were the first to set our hope on Christ, might live for the praise of his glory. In him you also, when you had heard the word of truth, the gospel of your salvation, and had believed in him, were marked with the seal of the promised Holy Spirit;

this is the pledge of our inheritance toward redemption as God's own people, to the praise of his glory. I have heard of your faith in the Lord Jesus and your love toward all the saints, and for this reason I do not cease to give thanks for you as I remember you in my prayers. I pray that the God of our Lord Jesus Christ, the Father of glory, may give you a spirit of wisdom and revelation as you come to know him, so that, with the eyes of your heart enlightened, you may know what is the hope to which he has called you, what are the riches of his glorious inheritance among the saints, and what is the immeasurable greatness of his power for us who believe, according to the working of his great power. God put this power to work in Christ when he raised him from the dead and seated him at his right hand in the heavenly places, far above all rule and authority and power and dominion, and above every name that is named, not only in this age but also in the age to come. And he has put all things under his feet and has made him the head over all things for the church, which is his body, the fullness of him who fills all in all.

ALL SAINTS DAY
LUKE 6:20-31
DANIEL 7:1-3, 15-18; PSALM 149; EPHESIANS 1:11-23

BLESS THE WORLD

A phone rang on a Sunday morning in September 1959. It broke into the joyful chaos that is life with five children between the ages of three and fourteen. It was a phone call she knew was coming, but that fact never does prepare one fully for the reality. It was the phone call that told her that her beloved husband, her soulmate, the father of her children, was dead at the age of 38. The brain tumor that had taken his health and vitality and had even begun to take his personality had taken his life.

Breaking into the silence of an empty nest, a phone rang in the summer of 1972. She thought it might be one of her kids calling or perhaps her surgeon husband calling to say he was on his way home. It was the phone call that told her that those swollen lymph nodes she had noticed were not the lingering effects of a winter cold: they were cancer.

A phone rang in a farmhouse kitchen on a cold January morning in 1990. The nurse on the other end confirmed what she already knew in her heart. Her husband of 27 years had died in the night. His body had given out. The cancer that had spread throughout his body and sent him into a coma had taken his life.

The portable phone on the end table next to the couch rang on a fall afternoon in 2003 and interrupted the quiet solitude of an afternoon spent knitting and reading. It was her doctor on the line. The biopsy results were back. She had lymphoma.

These four phone calls all came to the same woman. And each time she hung up the phone, she had a choice. When she lost her parents or had to endure the pain of watching her own children or grandchildren suffer, she had a choice. Her choice was to let that piece of news, that painful, horrible loss be the defining event of her life or to look around her and be grateful. If she chose the former it would be the lens through which she viewed the world and she would let tragedy define her. It would be a lens that would be a source of stress and worry. It would be an approach that would mean she would always be waiting for the other shoe to drop. It would be an approach that would not add hours to her span of life but instead would diminish the quality of her life.

Or if she chose the latter, if she chose gratitude, then she could celebrate the life and joys of her children. She could be an active and involved mother who continued to play tennis and take her children to the lake in the summer. She could marry again and spend the happy years of her husband's retirement living on a farm in Maine. She could be the host to her grandchildren for countless summers, reading to them, teaching them about the farm, and about their own family history. She could be a great-grandmother who moved to an apartment in the city to be nearer to her family and to be able to watch her great-grandchildren learn to walk.

The woman on the receiving end of these phone calls was my grandmother. She died in the spring of 2013 at the age of 92. She was a woman who dealt with a significant amount of personal tragedy, and who chose to let her life be defined by its many blessings rather than its tragic losses.

Today is All Saints Day and it is a day on which we remember those we have lost — those who have been "saints" in our lives and in our faith, those who have been examples and inspirations to us on our own faith journeys.

In our gospel this morning, Luke tells us that those who are poor or hungry or mourning are blessed because they will be provided for and comforted. Luke tells us not to fight back when we are persecuted, but rather to overcome challenges with kindness and gentleness. We have the classic passage that reminds us to "turn the other cheek" if we are struck. I have often thought of these passages as being about direct confrontation — about the times when we are physically harmed by another person. But in reflecting on these passages in light of my grandmother's life, I realize they can be taken on a more metaphorical level. They are not just about the times in our lives when we have been persecuted or confronted by another human being, they are about any times in our lives when we have faced significant challenges, when we have struggled, when we have lost someone.

We can be blessed in the midst of our pain; we can overcome challenges with kindness and generosity. But this doesn't just happen by itself. It requires action on our part. It is a choice we make, just as my grandmother did. It is a choice we make to either let our lives be defined by what is missing, by the pain we have suffered and what we have lost, or to allow our lives to be defined by our blessings, by all the gifts and sources of joy we have.

Being blessed doesn't just automatically happen — it is like forgiveness; it may be freely offered by God, but it only has meaning in our lives if we accept it and live with gratitude for the gifts we have been given.

I am sure we all know people who have had moments of choosing loss, choosing pain. We have all had those times when we have preferred to stay in our own misery and discomfort because at least they are familiar and may make us feel more in control. We have had those times when hurt or anger have gotten the better of us. We've had those times when we feel that God or the world owes us because it is entirely unfair that we should have to suffer. The issue, ultimately, is not whether or not we have moments of being focused on our pain or our anger. We are right to be angry.

We are right to cry out in pain when we suffer. Sometimes life is horribly unfair. We lose jobs. We fail tests in school. Beloved young people die far before their time. Our bodies give out. We are faced with illnesses and our own mortality. Sometimes life is *really* hard. It is okay to be angry and it is okay to be sad. The issue is whether or not we stay in that place — whether we choose to let our anger and our pain get the best of us. The issue is whether we choose to let them blind us to all the gifts and blessings in our lives.

This is why I am so grateful for my grandmother and her incredible example of faith. She faced a great deal of loss and challenge in her life, but she never let them define her. Nor did she expect her life to go perfectly or be devoid of suffering. Those who do let loss define them, those who expect life to go just swimmingly, are the ones being warned in Luke's gospel today: "Woe to you who are full now, for you will be hungry. Woe to you who are laughing now, for you will mourn and weep. Woe to you when all speak well of you, for that is what their ancestors did to the false prophets" (Luke 6:24-26).

We will face challenges and difficulties in the course of our lives. It is best to come to grips with that fact and not live with the presumption that everything will go swimmingly. We will not always be full, laughing, or spoken well of. But that does not mean our lives will be overwhelmed by pain or challenge. No, we are people of faith. We believe in resurrection. We believe that the love of God is stronger than anything in this world, even death. As the psalmist says, "God is our refuge and strength, a very present help in trouble. Therefore we will not fear, though the earth should change, though the mountains shake in the heart of the sea; though its waters roar and foam, though the mountains tremble with its tumult" (Psalm 46:1-3).

As people of faith, we can choose to trust in God. We can choose to seek out our blessings. We can choose to live with gratitude. We can choose to follow the example of all the saints in our lives, all those who have been examples of strength and hope to us, by choosing to define our lives by joy and blessing rather than by pain and loss. The challenges will come, and it is by holding fast to our faith, to our hope, to the ever-present reality of love and blessings in our lives that we can overcome those challenges.

The world needs more people whose lives are defined not by pain and loss, but by love and blessing. The world needs more blessing. Let us give thanks this day for all those in our lives who have showed us what it is to bless the world with our lives. Let us go forth and do likewise. Amen.

Thanksgiving Day
John 6:25-35

When they found him on the other side of the sea, they said to him, "Rabbi, when did you come here?" Jesus answered them, "Very truly, I tell you, you are looking for me, not because you saw signs, but because you ate your fill of the loaves. Do not work for the food that perishes, but for the food that endures for eternal life, which the Son of Man will give you. For it is on him that God the Father has set his seal." Then they said to him, "What must we do to perform the works of God?" Jesus answered them, "This is the work of God, that you believe in him whom he has sent." So they said to him, "What sign are you going to give us then, so that we may see it and believe you? What work are you performing? Our ancestors ate the manna in the wilderness; as it is written, 'He gave them bread from heaven to eat.'" Then Jesus said to them, "Very truly, I tell you, it was not Moses who gave you the bread from heaven, but it is my Father who gives you the true bread from heaven. For the bread of God is that which comes down from heaven and gives life to the world." They said to him, "Sir, give us this bread always." Jesus said to them, "I am the bread of life. Whoever comes to me will never be hungry, and whoever believes in me will never be thirsty."

* * *

Philippians 4:4-9

Rejoice in the Lord always; again I will say, Rejoice. Let your gentleness be known to everyone. The Lord is near. Do not worry about anything, but in everything by prayer and supplication with thanksgiving let your requests be made known to God. And the peace of God, which surpasses all understanding, will guard your hearts and your minds in Christ Jesus. Finally, beloved, whatever is true, whatever is honorable, whatever is just, whatever is pure, whatever is pleasing, whatever is commendable, if there is any excellence and if there is anything worthy of praise, think about these things. Keep on doing the things that you have learned and received and heard and seen in me, and the God of peace will be with you.

THANKSGIVING DAY
JOHN 6:25-35
DEUTERONOMY 26:1-11; PSALM 100;
PHILIPPIANS 4:4-9

AN ATTITUDE OF GRATITUDE

My favorite yoga teacher ends each class with an invitation: "You are now free to roam the earth in an attitude of gratitude." An attitude of gratitude — those are wise words. Might the world be a different place, might the kingdom of God be more fully realized, if more of us lived that invitation? Like most wisdom, that invitation is found across traditions, and most assuredly, we Christians can affirm that Christ invites us to live our lives in gratitude.

There is no doubt that we each have much to be thankful for. Hopefully, we are in a position to be grateful for material benefits — houses, cars, clothes, electronic gadgets, and many more things. Hopefully we can be grateful for a roof over our heads, for meals to eat, and for beds in which to sleep. For most of us in the United States, the list of things we are fortunate to have could go on and on.

Plus there are the intangible gifts. We are thankful for the blessings of family and friends. We are thankful for those companions on the way who help us to live more deeply into our faith. There is that oh-so-precious gift that our Savior Christ has given us — the gift of salvation. Christ stretched out his arms upon the cross so that we might come within the reach of his saving embrace — so that we might understand more fully the depths of God's love for us. He sacrificed his life so that we might better see the path we are to follow. We do have so very much to be thankful for!

I love Thanksgiving — not only because it is a holiday that centers around a good meal that is savored in the company of family and friends, but predominantly because it is a holiday that asks or invites us to slow down, to take stock, and to give thanks for the blessings in our lives. Something I would imagine many of us do not do often enough. We could all use a pause, a break, a time to reflect on the blessings in our lives. I hope that for most of us, today is a good day. It is a day of joyful celebration. We give thanks for the gifts in our lives, and we celebrate Christ as our king who has freed us from the bonds of sin and death. On joyous days like this it is easy to make a list of all the things for which we are grateful.

But there are the not-so-joyous days, and even Thanksgiving may not be so joyous for some of us. There are the days when we have physical aches and pains that hold us back. We have days when sadness clouds our vision. There are those days when we are angry and despondent — days when we are much more aware of what is missing than what we have to be grateful for. What are we to do then?

We have a choice. We can choose darkness. We can choose sin and despair. Or we can choose light. We can choose gratitude. Yes, even in the midst of pain, we can choose gratitude. Because Christ's invitation to live with gratitude is not an invitation for sometimes. It is not an invitation to be lived out only on the days that are joyous — it is an invitation for always. We can live with gratitude each and every day.

This invitation is not offered lightly. It does not disregard the reality of sin in the world or the hardships we all face. Christ is not blind to the pain we suffer — he knows it only too well. Christ is inviting us to live with gratitude because he knows that there is always something to be grateful for.

Even if we lose our possessions, even if we lose a job, even if a dream is shattered, even if we lose someone we love, there is still something for which we can be grateful.

We can be grateful for the love of God we have come to know in Jesus Christ. No matter what happens, no matter how life changes, no matter how our lives are turned upside down — God does not change. God's love for us does not change. There is nothing on earth — not even death — that can ever separate us from that love.

Interestingly, it is often in our darkest moments — the moments when the pain of life narrows our vision — that we are made aware of God's abiding presence and unfailing love. As the General Thanksgiving in the *Book of Common Prayer* reminds us, we are also to give thanks for those disappointments and failures that lead us to acknowledge our dependence on God alone. We are dependent on God — utterly dependent on God — and the marvelous truth is that he is always right there when we need him. When we fall, he catches us. When we stumble, he helps us back up again. He is with us every step of the way. And that truth, my friends, is worthy of our thanksgiving.

Giving thanks is at the heart of our worship life as Christians. It is what we do every Sunday as we gather in this place. We give thanks to God for our blessings. We need that time. We need time to slow down, to reflect, and to give thanks.

Thanksgiving is an opportunity for us to do that with our families and friends, many of whom may worship in other places or not at all on Sunday mornings. Thanksgiving is an opportunity to push the collective pause button on the hectic pace of American life. That, in itself, is a gift, and ideally one which is a regular part of our own personal spiritual lives.

On this day, let us give thanks to God for the gifts in our lives, for the gifts God has freely given us. I invite you to hold onto the sense of gratitude for the tremendous blessings in your lives — and there are tremendous blessings in your lives. If you don't believe me, you aren't looking hard enough. We have all been given that most profound gift of

God's abiding and sustaining love that is with us always. May we hold fast to the knowledge of all the blessings in our lives, so that when we go out into the world and life returns to its hectic pace, we may go filled with the peace of God, so that our hearts and our spiritual lives are not hijacked by the temptations of the world. Christ has issued us an invitation to follow him and to live with gratitude. In following Christ, may we find ways to live with "an attitude of gratitude" this day and always. Amen.

www.ingramcontent.com/pod-product-compliance
Lightning Source LLC
Chambersburg PA
CBHW071750040426
42446CB00012B/2514